a planted seed

Grace Gachoki

BookLeaf Publishing

Presentation by *BookLeaf Publishing*

Web: www.bookleafpub.com

E-mail: info@bookleafpub.com

ISBN: 9789357442244

First edition 2023

To the young girl who did not know her voice was worthy to be heard, and her thoughts could be an art form.

But most importantly, to God, for carrying her during the times there were only one set of footprints in the sand.

ACKNOWLEDGEMENT

Thank you to all those who've shown love in the poetry community.
Thank you to those friends in my life I call family.
Thank you to my sister, SV.
Thank you to those who have given me a reason to love, fight and protect. You are my inspiration to write.

Thank you to God.

PREFACE

Finding new connections, learning from old ones whilst figuring out who you are is isolating, exhausting but most importantly, revolutionary. You haven't met the person you are in this moment before, and regardless of circumstances you deserve to be celebrated.

I wrote this as a promise to myself and to plant a seed for more to grow. Each day I sought inspiration and pushed myself to be dedicated. This collection is a mixture of writing prompts, writing challenges, impulsive thoughts, and old extracts that have allowed me to truly enjoy the process. It became a mind map with no clear destination, but luckily it's the journey that's important and the company you're blessed with that matters - so join me and be a part of something the beautiful.

As you read through this, I hope you connect and resonate. And whatever comes to mind, the last page is yours to create.

Elemental

I am water, I move with grace and cover lands.
I am fire, I set worlds ablaze, I destroy,
I mould with my bare hands.
I am made of the earth, roots blind to the human
eye,
Deeper than soul ties, as powerful as the space
between my thighs.
I travel through the wind, listen as my desires
float,
In the air and brush against your ear.
I am in the trees, on the surface of leaves,
I change with the seasons, grow even in times of
depletion.
I am found in the stars, apparent both in the sky
and your eyes.
I am as lonely as the moon, dependent on my
mood,
My light still serving others, despite being alone
and in the nude.
I am filled with wonder, such as the night sky.
I am as subtle, delicate as day light, you do not
notice when I pass by.
I am painted with the hues of sunrise, and
beautifully left to recreate at sunset.
I burn like the sun, on each side of the world.

Burning inside out, within myself,
For your warmth, for my comfort, for our end.
I am, truly, coming into my element.

Gifted by My No

I learnt to say no by protecting you first.
I learnt what was not good enough for you,
Is a standard I need to hold true,
And so, I learnt to say no by trusting you first.
My heart had no choice but to carry you,
As you burst through,
All the colours of the rainbow captured in your smile,
All that is good, centred inside a child.
Our values reflect all those who love us,
So, I found myself within you.

Overtime my reflection, apparent not only in your eyes.
But also in the way you tilt your head,
Walk on your toes or bite your cheek in the midst of your cheeky lies.
I unearthed that,
Places you cannot grow, our footsteps will not tread,
Pieces that can not be placed over time,
Will not disturb our peace of mind.
Empty promises that carry no weight,
Will not be the rock upon which we wait.

I’ve learnt to say no by honouring the space you create.

Cook

She dances with the spoon,
Floats from one side of the room to the other,
Sprinkles seasoning guided by her ancestors,
Whilst creating a legacy of her own.
My bright eyes watch her with wonder,
As she cooks, my heart grows fonder.
It's a symphony of smells,
A dance alive on my tongue,
As she cooks, until the song is done.
Home is in the heart of those four walls,
Comfort present in the warmth of the pot,
As she cooks, my senses blend and unravel their knot,
Love, safety and time, forever in abundance,
As she cooks my pain away,
And I no longer suffer in silence.

I'd give you the world.

Looking at you is a reflection of myself, I see,
The hopes and fears you placed in me.
I see what I am, what I could've been.
I feel the weight of words unsaid,
Our silence misplaced in history.
Me - bound by what is asked of me.
You - anchored by there being only one of me.

Yet, I'd give you the world if I could.
Raised in suffering, bound by strength.
You've become what's always been destined.
A fountain of blessings.

Looking at you is a reflection of what I aim to be.
I see, love prevail unexpectedly.
I'm in awe of your capacity to love,
For lists of people who do not list your name.
But you do so willingly, and say it's to protect your daughters name.
She once said "Grace, nakupenda sana, God forbid there's a time you're in pain. I'd want to know you're coveted by the deeds I do in Jesus' name'

How do you measure that kind of love?
Is giving you the world, really enough?

It's A Good Day

At one point, a collective will open their eyes at the same time.
The dawn of a new day on their mind.
We will breathe in a sunrise,
And out, what I call, a warrior sigh.
You may still have the fight of yesterday,
But the promise of a new day,
Is testament to your resilience,
Persistence, to see beauty in the everyday.
Hope reflected in the colours of the sky,
As you walk with faith, that you're blessed by the most High.

3AM in London

Life slows down for a little while,
Streets are empty to give you space to empty
your mind.
You find a pocket of peace, as you stand still
with time.
There is a sense of intimacy, a type of delicacy
between you and passers-by.
All alone in this together, street maps and boris
bikes as your guide.
You take a deep breath, and centre yourself as
you refocus on 'why'.

Wishful thinking travels through the air,
As you dare yourself to think of possibilities you
will to come true.
The world is still moving, yet in this moment
there's only you,
And the inevitable truth, that all that matters is
your view,
Of the world, your sense of self, your heart at
present.
Who you decide to bless with your presence.
How you shine as bright as the nightlights, and
the sun in a few hours,
And even though the world is quiet,

You know, your essence speaks volumes and is what holds true power.

Tug of War

Let me illustrate a story.
Two strangers.
Both on opposite sides of the same idea,
Both living their lives with no idea,
That their choices are internally bound.

One can ascertain a path,
And that's where the other dreams to be found.
They both believe in trusting the process,
But one is focused on the journey, whilst the other on success.

They misinterpret this pull as the force of gravity,
Concluding this tug of war is the lack of consistency,
Between heart and mind.
Where one is grounded, and the other floats on cloud nine.
But in reality,
They're pulled by each other's sense of clarity,
And insanity, lies in their pursuit of perfect balance.

Your Personal Best

I forget myself in the sound of your voice.
My body is drawn to your lack of choice,
To be subtle, to be easy with me.
I like how your edges are rough, but it's the softness of your tip,
That I get to touch.
Legs wrapped, tongue tied, and bodies intertwined,
My heart beats to the rhythm of your strokes.
Thoughts scattered like our clothes,
On the bedroom floor.
Lost in the rhythm, as I go on all four.

I flirt with the line, below your waist,
Knowing it's a waste of time,
To stop the trajectory of my mind.
That shows me laid out, breathless,
My breast, your mouth, helpless.
To what comes next,
Your personal best.
I see your lips moving down,
And I'm like baby you are a G,
Spot, the quiver in my thighs, the rise in my chest
As I let go of whatever I had left.

Anticipate

Your touch.
Your words.
Your lips on mine.
There's pain in waiting.
Agony in tension.
I'm frozen in this state,
As I anticipate,
Your next move.

We've become finalists in this dance,
Flirting with the line, determined not to miss our chance.
Both on opposite sides, trying to read each other's mind.
Neither one of us willing to take one for the team,
Both loosing and questioning what our lives could've been.
And whether it's too late.
As I anticipate,
Your next move.

A part of me is tired,
Of holding back, holding on.
Our dance has turned into a competition,

And honestly, I am ready to accept the loss.
If that's the cost, for us to communicate.
So, here I stand.
White flag, surrender to this debate.
Of love, lust, passion or hate.
As I anticipate,
Your next move.

Free Course Meal

It's an early sunrise.
The steam from your coffee cup.
Is the fog over my eyes, from your bullshit lies.
I tilt my head, brush my lips on yours and as always, internalise.
I lay my head on your shoulder, take a bite out of breakfast pizza.
And feel at peace for a little while,
Before the world wakes up, and our love is on trial.

There you go again.
Making an ass out of you and me,
Assuming you can,
Mind read the roadmap that my thoughts travel across.
Only for us to come full circle,
It's a vicious cycle.
You think love means I offer parts of me on a platter for you to carve.
Whilst I stand there and polish the knife that you use to pick me apart.
I watch the blood trickle from the side of your mouth,

And your beautiful smile widen, exposing blood stained teeth that shine so bright,
Because you know despite, the excruciating pain.
I'll do it again and again and again.

I'm the icing on your cake,
The whipped cream to your hot chocolate.
First to touch your lips,
Last on your mind.
It's easy for you to find,
A reason to stay,
It's hard for me, because you're my sugarcane.
Sweet to taste, but effort to penetrate,
And the aftertaste, isn't worth the bittersweet memory fade.

The Aftermath

Everyone is telling me contacting you is a bad idea
That reaching out, is stepping back.
I risk a healing process, becoming an enemy of progress
But I don't have a blueprint for healing
Not when you were my first everything

Now what?
I did the unspeakable, the unreasonable,
And it was anti climatic.
Self destructive yet scarily realistic.
You've been knocked off,
The pedestal I placed you upon.
But now what?
If point A was you and point B was what could be.
The connection we had, again, is lost on me.
How do I illustrate our journey?
Where do my fantasy scenarios reside?
Where can my irrational thoughts hide?
Your potential can not paint our story
It just blurs the lines of my reality.
I thought I was doing this for you, us, the slight possibility,
But it just unveiled denial and led to clarity.

Killing Me Softly

Moving on seems idealistic, borderline self destructively optimistic.
But I do not believe love or potential love is supposed to feel so restrictive.
Creating distance will be in the form of small smiles and missed side glances,
As I try and form a boundary that significantly reduces our chances.
You see, I heard he sang a good song, I heard he had a style.
And so I was lost and fucked up for a long long while.
For an intense standstill in time, we flirted with the possibility.
To live something we actually believe, in a world that poisoned my sensitivity.
I have to come to terms with what I am letting go,
Right now, I do not believe, but I know it'll help me grow.
The feelings I developed, helped shape my idea of 'I love you',
He helped me build the picture, of my forever and 'I do'.
But reality set in, and turned my potential world upside down,

My heart is in pieces, yet I hope my realisation
realigns my crown.

When I think about what was, and what was lost,
Your company, your laugh and our conversation
is what I miss the most.
As I walk away, and close the door on what we
could be,
I'm torn between what I deserve, what I want
and what is right for me.
You seemed to fit so easily in my comfort whilst
also disturbing my peace.
You are on my mind, often. My feelings are
visible and so are the keys,
To the lock on my vulnerabilities.
I've romanticised you in my mind, you are the
figure that keeps me awake,
That plays the lead in the productions where my
heart is at stake.
But regret and disappointment, brings me back
to reality.
Because you do not meet my expectations, and
that is when I pray for clarity,
I am not convinced of who I am to you, and I
cannot risk second guessing,
You've unlocked a part of me, that wants more.
But baby, your uncertainty feels like I'm
trespassing.

None the Wiser

Time will tell.
Time has told, time and time again the same stories we've been sold.
Lines and lines of Black faces sentenced and visualised in chains,
As they say our people are the ones who need to change their ways.
But the burden of proof falls on those who aim to exclude,
Not those innocently hoping for you to include.

Let's start with our young Black kings,
How do we shield them from things,
Too big to understand.
To unclench their hands,
That's been made into fists,
Because society insists, they need to fight.
Just to make a stand.

How do we keep their innocence intact,
A place where vulnerability and curiosity are a thing of sun, light and wonder.
Not weapons to be used against them,
Or a cage to trap their thunder.

A young Black boy enters this world with a smile,
He's separate from whose may take a while.
This young Black boy is poured into with love,
Love is personified in his parent's provision, in the eyes of his little brother and the embrace of his big sister.
He has dreams of being a lawyer and professional footballer.
Because his dreams have no limits.
There is nothing he can not try.
He walks with his head held up high,
One-two stepping on a road, determined only by him and his mind eye.
Do you know how this story ends? What happens next?
Stepped on by society's humbleness.
Disguised as an act of kindness,
Because lest he believe he's greater than their perception.
The price to build and invest in his elevation,
Is too high.
Give him less than an inch, to ensure he doesn't reach that mile.
Silence his voice and provide the illusion of choice.
Then question the origin of his anger, the misplacement of his character,

When his box cannot contain him no longer,
when he becomes bigger than your big picture.
Your response – he has a chip on his shoulder.
His ego is bruised.
This is a story, we’ve already seen.
He thought too much of himself,
When, in reality, he just dared to dream.

Old Oak Tree

My heart, soul and eyes have cried for days.
But my grief does not account for lives lost, or
for those who refuse to change their ways.
Injustice has become rooted in our world,
creating a tale as old as time.
Planting the seed of prejudice to grow as tall as
an oak tree,
Where Black men were hung for their skin
colour crime.

There were generations of Black men who
fought for the freedom to choose when to sleep,
eat, or kiss their child goodnight.
There were generations of Black men who
wanted to live longer, and thought they could,
despite what reality was in sight.
There were generations of Black men who beat
the odds and told their story.
And watched as it was portrayed, to give the
white man the glory.

There are generations of Black men who serve
the death penalty because of the colour of their
skin.

There are generations of Black men who have been whipped, beaten, and abused because their Blackness is considered the ultimate sin.
There are generations of Black men who are incarcerated, belittled, and dehumanised because they dare to live life.
Not a life that defies the odds or deems them a survivor.
But an ordinary one that is hopeful and absent of strife.

There will be generations of Black men, whose innocence has an extremely early expiry date.
They will play with their toys, struggle with their math homework, and ask unnecessary questions.
Yet do not know their skin colour determines a future that others create.
There will be generations of Black men, who would like to explore every avenue that life has to offer.
But are subjected and bound to unwritten rules, by a white society that forces them to suffer.
There will be generations of Black men, who do not know that finding a job, getting married, passing their driving test are privileged struggles compared to taking a breath.

How do we tell our Black men, that their basic human function can be so callously denied and may lead to their death?

The power to end a life by denying the basic right to breathe,
Frightens me, because this hate grows so strong that it's determined to make every Black mother grieve.
Mothers to be, mothers that are, mothers that were, mothers that have daughters, aunties you call mum, mothers of mothers.
All those that saw the potential in the Black men, that could've been fathers and brothers.

This world we live in, prides itself in reckoning and revolution.
Yet it was built on the back of systemic and institutional racism.
This injustice is rooted as deep as an oak tree and helped build the foundation of this imperfect system.
Creating a world underneath that we cannot see,
Until the earth can contain it no longer, and the truth breaks free,
The branch like lies covered by blood-stained leaves.
Standing tall, and in plain sight, we recognise, it has always been,
The same century old oak tree.

CBT

I constantly commit the ultimate sin,
To myself.
I hold myself back in times of highs, and refuse to hold myself in times of lows.
I forget to celebrate, but remember to criticise.
Then I'm surprised, at the lack of belief I demonstrate on a daily basis.
My potential is seen more in the eyes of others, friends, lovers,
Than in the eye of the beholder, and that hurts.
Because who will be looking back at me when I'm older?
Will I be able to trust my reflection?
Sought validation from those who love you, still doesn't ground you.
Words of praise do not always elevate you, if the only time you hear them are on the lips of others.
You are not made whole by the perception of you, regardless of pure intent.
Your words, opinion and voice are always relevant, in every space, every continent.
As much as it helps, it's not another's responsibility to create a place for you at their table.

What would happen if I were to speak purpose
and truth into my life?
Instead of trying to find it elsewhere.

The Right Replayed Record

I am too beautiful to personify your
misconception.
I am too worthy to walk a path used to rejection.
My light shines too bright to be dimmed by your
shadow.
Greatness was a concept already foreshadowed,
Before my conception, that I stand here as a
manifestation,
Of Black excellence, and a thousand
possibilities.
The power I possess lifts me beyond heights, it
breaks limits and shatters ceilings.
I am crowned by the most High,
Destined to live abundantly in life.
Destined to give and receive love.
Destined to be more than enough.

It is not shameful to be proud of my essence.
To know I serve others, just by my presence.
I arrive in every space, with pure intention,
I do not give power to thoughts that shine a light
on another's imperfections.
And so, I am blessed beyond comprehension.

It is not shameful to be proud of my essence.

Because the most important lesson, is to lead with compassion.
A lesson that starts within.
It creates a supernatural force, that separates the losses from the wins.
Imagine - to think, at times, I do not know what I am capable of.
When I was born with the capacity to love, planted in me from God above.

Arise

I stand before you as a confident Black woman.
I think. Maybe
I stand before you as a Black woman. But I'm
soft spoken, I don't know how to do my hair and
I sometimes listen to Taylor Swift.
I stand before you as a woman.
But do I want to though?
Will you be interested in the contents of mind, if
you can see the curves of my body.
I stand.
Because that is all I know how to do in the face
of adversity.

Society has already strapped on the restraints of
similarity, and has the straight jacket ready in
case we ever manage to break free.
Our identity stripped and stolen.
What do you want from me?

Politicians, policies and false prophets perceive
you powerless,
But their power lessens when you use your
voice,
They will tell you don't look in the mirror, you
won't like what you see.

But lift your gaze.
Hold your head up higher.
Breathe and count to three.

Don't you know you are a queen?
That you have the heritage of the kings of kings.
God said no weapon formed against you shall prosper.
You are covered and blessed by his Grace.
So, why do you walk in the shade as if to cover your face?

Don't you know you were raised by a queen?
Her strength and love shaping your very being.

Don't you know you have the ancestry of powerful African kings and queens,
Who were taken from their great civilisation, bound by oppression yet fought for the freedom of their future generation?

Don't you know - then I realise.

I am only confined by the limits of my mind.
Like my hair, I am not meant to be tamed,
I owe it to myself and those who stood before me, to stand unashamed.

And so you, out there can attempt to empathise,
victimise maybe even sympathise.

But like the Queen Maya Angelou said,
Still I rise.

That Girl

It starts with an uncertain stare, a glare, a look
up and down.
Followed by the tilt of the head, and a barely
unnoticeable frown.
They are the innocent fish, in these shark
infested waters.
They open their mouth, as if to ask a question.
But quickly close it to avoid suspicion.
Yet this does not stop them, it's as if it's too
much.
The words are rising, choking them as if they
might just throw up.
It's almost an injustice, not to say what's on their
mind.
These oppressors of humankind.
"No offence but…"
No you did mean offence you narrow-minded
fool.
Am I just supposed to stand here, whilst you
indirectly attack my ancestry pool?
"Why are you getting so mad?"
Because I am ashamed.

I am the who girl who sat quietly as her teacher
told her she had to remove her braids, because
they weren't part of the school uniform.
I am the girl who laughed and joked with the
white boy, who blamed my Blackness for his
missing pen.
I am the girl who once stated she does not date
Black men.
I am the girl who treated her skin, as something
she should be ashamed in.
I am the girl who did not accept her curves,
culture or natural hair.
Because it was seen as a burden too big to bear.
Because it separated me from the crowd,
highlighted my difference.
And meant I suffered in silence.

The price I paid, for words unsaid, has distorted
my peace of my mind.
I wish I could travel back in time, and hold that
girl with the broken pieces.
Hold her hand, and tell her, even if she doesn't
feel like she belongs, she is still strong.
There is no need to dull your light, or intellect,
To suit the needs of others, who do nothing but
project their insecurities.
Because they simply do not understand, how one
person can shine so bright despite inequalities.
I wish I forgave her earlier,

For being a passer-by in her own story, when she had main character energy.

Now,
I am the girl whose found her community.
I am the girl who laughs wholeheartedly, and hums when she's happy.
I am the girl who does not accept she is not Black enough,
Because I do not need to fit into your box, in order to be loved.
I am the girl who accepts the way her hair rises, to create her crown.
I was the girl who cried herself to sleep, praying to find somewhere to belong.
Who tried to find her worth in a boy, or the lyrics of a song.
I thought the answer to who I am, was on the tongues of those who degraded me.
Not understanding it was in the Bible and on the pages of Black history.

A You Problem

You've mistaken her with the reflection of her
past,
Distorted through time,
Misplaced in history,
Pulled apart.
Her true nature a mystery.

You've mistaken her for who you were used to,
The figure moulded to suit you,
When her edges were softened, eager to people
please,
Holding her breath, to put you at ease,
Failing to take risks,
At the risk of falling.

Now,
You're surprised when you are cut,
By her rough newly formed edges.
She's the rose with the thorns,
Before her imperfections were severed,
Before she misplaced what was treasured.
You look at her like your hurt should cause her
to bleed,
When your only role was to feed off her fear.
You're surprised at her distance,

Which replaced her persistence,
To keep you by her side.
Now, your misery misses her company,
As she walks without your liability.

Dear 2023,

I want to chase sunsets in every lifetime,
Capture sunrises in the palm of my hands,
Live a life of peace, sans complacency,
Listen to the wind whisper delicately, as it
uplifts me.
Rise above negativity, and insecurity,
Believe in my promise, potential and prosperity.
Love who I am, and how I was made.
Avoid chaos, unhealthy attachments, and words
unsaid.
Turn the tide in my favour.
Invest in myself, and trust my saviour.
I am a blessing, formed by The Almighty.
My path is not to be tread lightly,
Or with caution.
I promise to arrive in my full authenticity,
Covered with His Grace, and blessed with
creativity.

Title:

your space to create.

www.ingramcontent.com/pod-product-compliance
Lightning Source LLC
Chambersburg PA
CBHW051743130826
49812CB00033B/982